GULF COAST COLONIALS

A Compendium of French Families in Early
Eighteenth Century Louisiana

by
Winston De Ville

With an Introduction by
James Daniel Hardy, Jr.

CLEARFIELD

Copyright © 1968 by Winston De Ville
All Rights Reserved.

Permission for reproduction in
any form may be secured
from the editor.

Genealogical Publishing Company, Inc.
Baltimore, Maryland
1968

Reprinted for
Clearfield Company, Inc. by
Genealogical Publishing Co., Inc.
Baltimore, Maryland
1995, 1999

Library of Congress Catalogue Card Number 68-9400
International Standard Book Number: 0-8063-0093-0

Made in the United States of America

GULF COAST COLONIALS

OTHER BOOKS BY WINSTON De VILLE

Colonial Louisiana Marriage Contracts, Volumes I - V
Louisiana Colonials: Soldiers and Vagabonds
Acadian Church Records, Volume I
Calendar of Louisiana Colonial Documents, Volumes I - II
Louisiana Troops, 1720-1770

Detail from "Veuë du Camp de la Concession de Monseigneur Law au Nouveau Biloxy," 1720, showing the warehouse and cabins in the background. A copy of the original print is at the Newberry Library, Chicago.

TABLE OF CONTENTS

	Page
Foreword	9
Introduction	11
The Colonists	17
The Priests	65
Index	67

FOREWORD

Genealogists and historians in colonial Louisiana studies have long felt the need of published vital statistics for the thorough study of the French in the Mississippi Valley and on the Gulf Coast. This publication, utilizing copies of WPA records of baptisms, marriages, and funerals for most of the earliest Louisiana families, attempts to fill this academic gap.

It is not unlikely that the typescripts used for this study contain typographical mistakes in spelling and in dates – a fact that magnifies the deplorable condition and availability of records in the French South. Good scholars have many opportunities and subjects that demand their attention. They are, then, quickly disabused by the various stumbling-blocks in this area of historical concentration. Consequently, this work does not purport to be definitive; it is merely a guide – a tool to intrigue the serious researcher to continued investigations.

The book is organized into family groups, usually headed by the male member, followed by the spouse – both in large type. Children are listed last, in relative order of birth. As the groups are alphabetized according to the male's family name, only the spouses appear in the index. It was necessary to standardize spelling – a practice usually frowned upon by this writer – but variations are given when they appear to be significant.

The editor is very grateful to Jim Hardy for his valuable contribution, placing this record in proper historical perspective.

           Winston De Ville
           O. M. P. L.

November 8, 1967
811 Orleans Street
New Orleans

INTRODUCTION

In old regime France, the Catholic church held an imposing position in state and society. It was the King's faith and the state church. Louis' subjects were supposed to follow their monarch in matters of religion and be good Catholics. They were expected to attend mass, pay their tithes and dues, and resort to the church at the crucial junctures of their lives. Frenchmen should be baptized, married, have their children baptized, and be buried as Catholics. They were legally obligated to do so. A marriage performed anywhere but a Catholic church was invalid, and the parties were living in sin. Their children were illegitimate, their will and contracts unenforceable at law. Babies not given Christian baptism were not people, and their births were unrecorded. Those who declined Catholic burial could assume that their wills would be questioned in court. With such sanctions, who could wonder that the people went to their priest to be married, buried or have their children baptized as Christians.

It was not merely the duty of the priest to officiate at these ceremonies and mysteries, he must also record them. The obligation to keep these parish records was rigorously enforced by the state, which made up the taille and impositions rolls from them. The priests were dragooned into being the recorders for the state. Thus the parish records are one of the most important single sources for information on the common people of the old regime. Population figures and trends can only be determined with any accuracy from the parish records. The social structure of the community can

be gleaned from the church records. Social mobility, or the
lack of it, appears in the parish archives. Wars, famines,
epidemics and other disasters show in the church records
more clearly, and in more detail, than in any other source.
And finally, the church archives are indispensible for any
geneological research.

This is as true for Mobile as Paris, though Mobile was
the most distant outpost of empire in the French eighteenth
century colonial system. Lacking the habitants of Canada, or
the rich sugar crops of the islands, Mobile was essentially a
military outpost. Its few settlers were poor and humble, almost
always of peasant origin, sometimes convicts. In the
Mobile parish records we will not find a Richelieu, baptized
with ceremony in the hopes of a great career in the royal service,
or even a Robespierre, whose humble birth gave no hint
of future renown. Mobile was too poor, too small, too far
away from the seats of government, trade, or the church.
But there were differences among the inhabitants of the colony,
differences of class, birth, occupation, which were magnified
and frozen into a social ladder by the very remoteness of the
area. The church records illuminate these as no other source
can.

The Mobile aristocracy was the army officers and the
priests, both being occupations officially privileged in the old
regime. The officers often added noble, or at least gentle,
birth to their rank. Thus captain Marchand was listed as a
squire. Francois Philippe de Mandeville was the commandant
of Mobile, and a knight of Saint-Louis, as was Jean-Paul Le
Sueur, the town major. By the standards of metropolitan
France these were petty provincial nobles, too poor and ill-
connected to avoid service in the colonies, or buy positions in

fashionable regiments. But in Mobile, they were the great of this world. They hardly needed the juridical privileges accorded to the second estate. Their military rank, their gentle birth, their salary in gold, their access to the governor, their marriage alliances to the large land-owners; all of these things gave the regimental officers a social position so exhalted that no mere soldier or habitant could hope to compete. Less privileged, but still definitely in the aristocracy, were the priests and garrison chaplains. Like the noble officers, they too possessed the legal advantages of belonging to a privileged estate. And, like the officers, theoretical privilege provided only small support for their station. The clerk's real power came from his connections in France, with his brother Jesuits, Capuchins, or missionary society. Who was rash enough to offend a man who could reach such personages as Cardinal Fleury, Cardinal Bernis, or the devout Dauphin? Official support and esteem, both in New Orleans and in France, counted for more in creating a colonial aristocracy than legal honors.

In the middle of the tiny colonial society came the merchant, trappers, artisans and small farmers. At home, there would have been a gigantic social gap between the bourgeois merchants, the lower middle class artisans and the peasant farmers. But this was not France, and none of these activities produced an income widely different from the others. All of these occupations commended themselves equally to the military and religious authorities, as being useful and valuable to the colony. None of these people were rich, none of these occupations very far out of a barter economy. But the farmer, artisan and merchant were propertied, and received the modest status given in the old regime to small landholder and the technically skilled.

At the bottom of the ladder were the slaves and those recently freed. In a society as small as Mobile, lacking the great sugar and tobacco plantations of the islands, it was possible for the royal policy of Christianizing the Indian and Negro slaves to have some meaning. Further, there was considerable cohabitation between French owners and their slaves. Thus Jean Bigorre had a natural son by his Indian slave Angelique. The son, Francois, was, of course, baptized. The merchant, Charli, had a son by his Indian slave, as did Pierre Renauld. The children of these unions, and their slave mothers, and the slaves brought into the colony as laborers, these formed the lowest social class in Mobile.

There was no period in its colonial history in which Mobile did not contain more soldiers than any other occupation. The soldiers themselves ranked above the slaves, certainly, but considerably below the landed peasants or the skilled artisans. Partly, this was due to their profession, which was considered particularly degrading in the old regime. But very largely, it was the soldiers themselves. Army recruiting was done mainly by impressement or jail delivery, and the ranks were filled with criminals, debauchees, smugglers, idlers and vagabonds. The worst food, the most callous and indifferent treatment sufficed for these men. The most brutal discipline, enforced by the knout and fist, kept the troops in line. In Mobile, as elsewhere, they were seldom allowed powder and shot, for fear they would murder their superiors. Yet, all things considered at Mobile, the troops received a better life than they would have in a French garrison town. In the colony, many married, and some even ultimately became farmers, lifting themselves into the ranks of the respectable and propertied.

In organization and function, the colony of Mobile was a military outpost, to an extent that completely overwhelmed any agricultural and commercial pursuits that it may have boasted. Mobile simply lived off the soldiers and their officers. Thus, the tiny outpost did not resemble the typical French garrison town of the metropole, in which the army was a subsidiary form of income and a major cause of trouble and disturbance. It was more nearly like a Roman military encampment on the fartherest frontier of empire; a fort around which a small group of peasants, traders and artisans huddled for support and protection.

It is, of course, easy enough to describe Mobile as a poor and squalid little fort, but nothing makes this essential fact so stark and clear as the church records. Winston De Ville has done historians, sociologists and geneologists an immense service by this publication of the Mobile records, one of the two or three major sources for the history of that community. Mr. De Ville knows more about the archival resources for the French period in the lower Mississippi Valley and the Gulf Coast than anyone now working in the period, and it is fitting that these documents should be edited by him.

         James D. Hardy, Jr.
         Assistant Professor of
         History, L. S. U.
         O. M. P. L.

Baton Rouge, 1967

THE COLONISTS

JOSEPH ABREMAK - Swiss soldier; buried 13 August 1760.

JEAN ALEXANDRE - Master joiner.
MARIE MARGUERITE DUFRENE (DU FRESNE)
    FRANCOIS - Born 11 April 1708.
    PHILIPPE - Born 20 July 1710.
    ANTOINE - Born 1 September 1715.
    PIERRE - Born 21 November 1717.

JEAN BAPTISTE ALEXANDRE - Creole of Mobile
FRANCOISE HYPPOLITE BODIN - Creole of Mobile; buried 3 June 1744.
    JEAN BAPTISTE - Born 10 May 1734.
    CHARLES - Born 30 December 1736.

VINCENT ALEXANDRE - Habitant of Fort Louis.
MARIE PROT
    ANNE - Born 11 March 1709.

PHILIPPE ALIN - Buried 25 April 1763.

FRANCOIS ALVIN - Master arquebusier, died 9 October 1738, 45 years old, native of Corbeille, parish of St. Leonard, archbishopric of Paris, son of Francois Allevin, also a master arquebusier, and Magdelaine Gibier.
    CATHERINE CHRISTOPHE - Buried 16 January 1735.

FRANCOIS ALVIN
    MARIANNE - Francois Alvin's Indian slave.
    JEAN FRANCOIS - Born 30 November 1721.
    FRANCOIS - Baptized 1724. (Note: At the time of baptism, the father declared this child and his mother free.)

FRANCOIS AMOND
MARGUERITE COLON
    JEANNE MARGUERITE - Baptized 23 January 1738; buried 24 February 1738.

BERTRAND ANDRÉ

17

ELIZABETH BERNARD
(Daughter) - Baptized 17 November 1724.

FRANCOIS ARBILLAUD - Swiss soldier, native of Joinville; buried 15 July 1754.

JEAN AREDRAY
MARIE SULIVAN - Native of Ireland; died 9 July 1766.

LOUIS ASSALY (ASSAILLEY) dit FRANCHE MONTAGNE - Native of Niord, parish of St. André, diocese of Poitiers. Married 1 May 1724, to
    MARIE THERESE BRET - (Niece ?) of Michel Sorot; native of La Rochelle, parish of Notre Dame. (Note: On some records, her name is spelled BRY.)
    (Daughter) - Baptized 14 August 1724.
    JOSEPH CLAUDE - Born 1 August 1726.
    MARIE THERESE - Baptized 6 July 1728.
    ANNE - Born 3 April 1732.
    JEAN BONAVENTURE - Born 20 October 1734.
    MARIE - Born 12 January 1737

THOMAS ASSELIN
(Thomas Asselin's Indian Slave)
    ELIZABETH - Baptized 20 September 1736.

THOMAS ASSELINNE - Native of the parish of Fleuru in Basse-Normandy, diocese of Coutance. Married 12 January 1725, to
    MARIE FRANCOISE LANI (LAMI ?, LEMIR) - Native of the parish of Lubin, diocese of Vannes.
    MARIE - Baptized 28 September 1725.
    ETIENNE - Born 16 August 1727.
    (Daughter) - Born 18 December 1729.

AUBERGERON (BERGERON) - Killed by the Chÿs (Indians) in April 1739, near Fort Tombecbé while fishing in his pirogue.

AUBERT - Commandant at Fort Alibamons.
    LOUISE BERNOUDY - Buried 23 March 1759.

NOEL AUBERT - Soldier.
    MARIE MARGUERITE ROQUE.
    MARIE MARGUERITE - Born 21 May 1722

JOSEPH AUGERON - Soldier in De Merveilleux's company.

JEANNE VERGNE
    JEAN - Born 11 June 1729.
    MARIE JEANNE - Baptized 18 December 1730,
    "fille naturel et legitime."

PIERRE AUGERON - Soldier; son of Jean Augeron and Marie Devon; native of St. Pierre de Faulx, diocese of Tours; died 25 August 1747, 53 years old.

RENE AVRIL - Esquier, Sieur de la Vareine.
ANNE QUENTIN
    MARIE JEANNE - Born 3 October 1717.

PIERRE BAGLIN (BAGLEINE) - Soldier.
MARIE ANNE GABRIAU (GABRIEL)
    MARIE ANGELIQUE - Born 7 June 1719.
    PIERRE BARTHELEMY - Born 2 August 1720; died 10 September 1720.
    PIERRE - Born 10 November 1721.

JEAN BARAU - Native of St. George du Bois, province of Aulnix, bishopric of LaRochelle; died 31 May 1741.

JOSEPH BARBAU dit BOISDORE - Master-tailor; native of Quebec.
    JEANNE (LOUISE) BRET - Died 27 May 1747.
        JOSEPH ETIENNE - Born 23 February 1727.
        CLAUDE - Born 13 March 1729.
        LOUIS - Baptized 3 January 1731, "fils naturel et legitime."
        JEANNE LOUISE - Born 13 June 1732; Buried 2 September 1732.
        MARIE LOUISE - Born 7 November 1733.
        MARIE JOSEPH - Born 2 December 1735; died 4 November 1737.
        JEAN - Baptized 4 November 1737.
    (Note: Jean Claude Barbaux, undoubtedly one of the sons, was buried 5 March 1746.)
    (Note: Marie Therese Bret is the sister of JEANNE BRET, according to one record.)

IGNACE BARBET DE LA FERNE - Surgeon-major; died 4 June 1757, about 45 years old.

MARTIN BARDET - Soldier in La Tour's company.
    MARIE TACHOUNE (JOUVILLINAC)

CHARLES - Born 10 June 1721.
JULIEN - Born 16 November 1727.

VALENTIN BARREAU
    HYPOLITE MERCIER
    JEANNE MARGUERITE - Born 29 January 1708.

BALTHESAR BARTHELEMY
    MARIE MARGUERITE DUFRESNE (DE FRESNE)
    HENRY BALTHESAR - Born 20 September 1720.
    (Son) - Born 7 March 1723.

JEAN BAUDRAN dit VA DE BON COEUR - Soldier in Le Sueur's company; son of Louis Beauderan; native of Faubourg of Paris, parish of St. Paul; buried 8 May 1740.

JEAN BAPTISTE BAUDRAU - Creole of Dauphine Island; son of Jean Baptiste Baudrau dit Graveline of Pascagoulas and Susanne. Married 1 March 1734, to
    MARIE CATHERINE VINCONNAU - Native of La Rochelle; daughter of deceased Louis Vinconnau, master-tailor, and Catherine Donkin, whose second husband is Joseph Simon dit La Pointe of Pascagoula.

PIERRE DOMINIQUE BAYAUD - Son of Pierre Dominique Bayaot and Elizabeth Paquielte; Sergeant in Bombelle's company; died 8 October 1734.

AUGUSTIN BEAUGISSE dit LA LIME - Corporal; son of Augustin Beaugisse and Magdelaine Dechamp; native of Joigny in Bourgogne, diocese of Sens. Buried 24 November 1742.

JOSEPH BEAUVAIS - Buried 4 February 1764.

JOSEPH BECK - Sergeant in the Swiss Company; "Perit dans la traversée des Apalaches a la Mobile," 1 April 1762.

DOMINIQUE BELLZAGUY - Gunsmith of Paris.
    MARGUERITE HOUSSEAU (TOULOUSE) - Native of Chantilly.
        LOUISE MARGUERITE - Born 9 November 1720.
        LOUISE MARGUERITE - Born 29 November 1733.

JEAN BELSAGUY - Habitant of Mobile; native of Pelette, near Bayonne; son of Joannes Belsaguy "handy daguere," (of the diocese of Bayonne.) Died 7 April 1740.

BELEQUE
 (WIFE NOT GIVEN)
  MARIE MARTHE - Born 17 November 1752.

JEAN BERGE dit LA GRELE - Soldier; son of Bernard Berge and Susanne Plume; native of Valmond in Lorraine, diocese of Metz; mason by trade; died 6 February 1753.

BERNHOLD (?)
 BARBE (LAST NAME NOT GIVEN)
  ELIZABETH - Baptized in January 1725.

FRANCOIS BERNOUDY - "Procureur" for the king and Treasurer of Mobile; died 1 February 1757.

PIERRE BERTEN - Married 17 January 1726, to ANGELIQUE VEU - Native of Paris.

BERTHELOT - Gunsmith for the king.
 MARGUERITE PANYOUSSA - Buried 27 November 1746.

URBAIN BERTHELOT
 MARIE LEMIR
  JEAN - Born 12 August 1720.

RENÉ BESSON
 MARIE ANNE DE VALLÉE
  FRANCOIS - Born 6 June 1719.
  ANGELIQUE - Born 30 October 1720.

JEAN JACQUES BETAN - Swiss soldier; native of Bavoy, canton of Berne; buried 28 May 1735.

JEAN BAPTISTE BIDAU - Church-warden of Mobile; died 14 February 1754.
 HENRIETTE HUET - Died 9 February 1770.

FRANCOIS BIDOT dit LORAIN - Son of Nicolas Bidot and Marguerite Marinieve; native of Aubreville, parish of St. Martin; Buried 25 October 1737.

PIERRE (JACQUES) BIDOT dit ST. JACQUES - Soldier in Marchand's company; corporal in Beauchamp's company; Buried 12 December 1760.
 ANNE ROSE CHABERT
  CHARLE - Born 23 November 1727; Buried 11

December 1747.
JEAN PIERRE - Born 20 September 1730.
PIERRE - Born 26 September 1731; Buried 10 May 1733.
MARIE JEANNE - Born 17 February 1734.
LOUIS PIERRE - Baptized 19 August 1737; Buried 24 November 1739.
MARIE CATHERINE - Buried 25 November 1742.

JEAN BIGORNE
   ANGELIQUE - Indian Slave.
      FRANCOIS - Baptized 20 September 1731, "<u>fils indien naturel.</u>"

ANTOINE BLANCHET - Soldier; Buried 15 October 1757.

CLAUDE ANTOINE BLONDEL dit ST. HONORE - native of the parish of St. Parul, Paris; soldier in Beauchamp's company; Buried 20 October 1733.

NICOLAS BODIN - Native of Mont Louis, city, diocese, and archbishopric of Tours; Died 6 February 1746.
   FRANCOISE PAILLET - Native of the parish of Plemier, diocese of Vannes in Brittany.
      FRANCOISE HYPPOLITE - Born 11 October 1716.
      BERNARD - Born 17 April 1721.
      LOUIS FRANCOIS - Born 9 June 1722.
      MARIE LOUISE - Born 9 April 1725.
      MARIE ANNE JOSEPHE - Born 8 April 1727.
      MARTHE - Born 9 November 1730.
      MARIE LOUISE - Born 3 May 1734.
      JEANNE - Baptized 29 August 1737.
   (Note: Nicolas Bodin's "nickname" was MIRAGOUINE; this name is often used instead of his family name. Although one record dated 1721, styles him Nicholas Bodin, Sieur de Miragoine, it seems apparent that he was never ennobled.)

JEAN BAPTISTE BOHOM
   (WIFE NOT GIVEN)
      MARIE MARGUERITE - Baptized 15 December 1737.

RENE BOISSINOT - Soldier.
   ISABELLE (ELIZABETH) RUELLANT
      RENE - Baptized 2 January 1715.
      FRANCOIS RENE - Born 3 May 1716.

JEANNE ELIZABETH - Born 4 November 1719.
ELIZABETH) Born 26 April 1721. Twins
JEANNE)

JEAN BON - Gunsmith for the king; native of La Rochelle;
Buried 7 March 1736.

PIERRE BOUCHARD - Native of Montreal.
MARIE MARGUERITE ALEXANDRE - Creole of Mobile.
JOSEPH - Born 22 August 1736.

JOSEPH BOUDIGNON dit VIVARET - "Patron" for the king;
"Commis distributeur" at the Fort Condé warehouse.
ANNE CLERE POIRIER
PIERRE - Born 12 December 1729.
THEODORE - Born 11 March 1732; Died 11 September 1733.
ANNE MARGUERITE - Born 26 February 1734.
MARIE JOSEPH - Born 18 November 1735; Buried 10 September 1738.
FRANCOIS - Baptized 30 December 1737.

ANTOINE BOUETTE DE BLEMUR - Son of Jean Baptiste Bouette, Chevalier, Seigneur de Blemur, and Francoise Julienne Talon; native of the parish of Notre Dame de Piscop, diocese of Paris; Died 8 December 1739.

JEAN BOURBONNOIS
MARIE ELIZABETH DES HAYES
ELIZABETH ANGELIQUE - Born 17 August 1707.

JEAN BAPTISTE BOUREAU - Native of Besancon; corporal in Marchand's company; Died 1 July 1726.

GUILLAUME BOUTIN
LOUISE MARGUERITE HOUSSAU
NICOLAS - Born 23 December 1707
MARIE MARGUERITE - Baptized 19 January 1709.

BOUTTÉ
(NO WIFE GIVEN)
MARIE VERONIQUE - Died 8 March 1749.
JEAN CLAUDE - Died 11 September 1750, fourteen months old.

JEAN BRANCHU - Native of La Chapelle Ulain, bishopric of

Nantes; Died 22 November 1742.

AUGUSTIN BRANDSINGER - Native of Tarquen in Basse Alsace; Died 14 May 1735.

JACQUES BRANUT dit LA FRANCE - Native of St. Denis in France; sergeant of a detached company of the Marine; Buried 20 July 1733.

LOUIS DOMINIQUE BRET - Native of La Rochelle; Died 29 September 1744.

NICOLAS BREUN - Native of Equemine, bishopric of Besancon; soldier in a Swiss Company of Karrer's regiment; Died 15 September 1751.

ANTOINE BRION - Native of Daleman in Savoy, bishopric of Geneve; soldier in a Swiss Company of Karrer's regiment; Died 5 November 1750.

PIERRE BROSSARD - master mason.
    MARIE THERESE BROCHON
        PIERRE - Born 18 June 1708.
        FRANCOIS - Born 18 February 1710.

JEAN BRUDEL dit LA ROSE - Native of Lyon; son of Brudel, master joiner, parish of St. Paul; Died in February of 1733.

PIERRE BUCHWALTER dit DUBOIS - Native of Switzerland.
    LOUISE VALTERE
        (Son) - Born 3 October 1740; Died 3 October 1740.

JEAN GUILLAUME BURAT - Native of Saleure, diocese of Basle; married 11 May 1725; soldier; corporal in De Lusser's company; died 6 March 1736.
    MADELEINE ROGER (ROUGET) - Daughter of Mathieu Rouget; native of La Rochelle, diocese of La Rochelle.
        "FILS NATUREL ET LEGITIME" - Born 26 November 1728.
        JEAN PIERRE - Born 3 March 1733.

PIERRE CABIEN - Habitant of Fort Louis.
    FRANCOISE JALLOT
        MARIE GENEVIEVE - Born 1 September 1715.

FRANCOIS CAJOT - Died 21 April 1749.

(Note: One Jean Cajot, about 12 years old, was accidently killed in the woods and was buried 7 March 1764. There is no indication of relationship.)

JEAN CAN
  MAGDELAINE ROBERT
    JEAN FRANCOIS - Born 4 October 1704.

JEAN VALENTIN CANEL
  MARGUERITE PIERRE
    JEAN VALENTIN - Baptized 14 January 1723.

ANDRE CANNARD
  ELIZABETH BRENARD
    CLAUDE - Born 6 October 1721.

JEAN FRANCOIS CANSER dit CANELLE - Master carpenter in the king's service; Died 8 September 1741.
MARIE PRIEUR.

LOUIS CARLIER - Soldier; Buried 19 September 1760.

JEAN CARMOUCHE dit LORAIN - Locksmith for the Company.
  ANNE ALEXANDRE CHENET
    JEAN BAPTISTE - Baptized 27 May 1727.
    CLAUDE - Born 5 July 1729.
    JEAN BAPTISTE - Born 21 September 1731.
    ANNE - Baptized 14 November 1734.
    (Note: Robert Talon is listed as the children's uncle; Marie Praux, their grandmother.)

ANDRE CARRIERE
  MARIE MARGUERITE ARLU
    ANDRE - Born 30 July 1720.
    MARIE JOSEPHE - Born 26 January 1722.

FRANCOIS CARRIERE
  FRANCOISE JALLOT
    THERESE FRANCOISE - Born 16 March 1719.
    MARIE FRANCOISE - Born 4 February 1722.
    MARIE JOSEPHE - Baptized 1 January 1724.

JEAN CARRIERE - Native of Mobile; Died 3 September 1741, 18 years old.

CERINGE
(NO WIFE GIVEN)
CLAUDE - Died 29 August 1751.
ANNE MARIE - Died 30 August 1751.

FRANCOIS CHAMBRIE - Soldier in Grandchamp's company; died 9 October 1751.

CHARLI - Merchant
(Indian Slave of Charli)
NICOLAS - 11 August 1709.

FRANCOIS CHARNIER - Sergeant in Grandchamp's company; native of St. Agnes in Franche Comté; buried 10 October 1760.

NICOLAS CHATELIN - Habitant; drowned in the "Riviere des Apalaches" 3 March 1763.

FRANCOIS CHAUMONEAU - Son of Jean Baptiste Chaumoneau and Catherine la Ket; native of Guise in Picardy, diocese of Soissons; soldier in Benoist's company; died 12 October 1737, 21 years old.

JACQUES CHAUVIN
    MARIE ANNE DE LA VERGNE
        MARIE MAGDELAINE - Born 3 January 1715.
        JACQUES VINCENT - Born 9 January 1715. (Note: This entry was dated as shown, but listed with the 1727 baptisms.)

JOSEPH CHAUVIN dit DE LERY - Merchant at Fort Louis.
    HIPPOLITE MERCIER
        JOSEPH - Born 5 October 1709.
        MARIE ANTOINE - Born 23 February 1715.

CHRISTOPHE CHEVALIER dit ST. ONGE - Soldier in Bonnille's company; native of Jonsaque, diocese of Xaintes, shoemaker; died 2 March 1753.

JEAN ROBERT CHIERDEL dit MAISON NEUVE - Surgeon-major at Fort Condé; he was deceased by 1734.
    MARIE LANIER (L'AMI) (LAMY)
        MARIE ANNE - Born 30 March 1730; buried 27 April 1733.
        ANNE - Baptized 22 October 1732
        JEAN ROBERT - Born 17 December 1734; buried

10 May 1736.

IGNACE CHOLTZ dit BRISE BATAILLE - Soldier in Bertet's company; native of Scelestat, parish of St. George, bishopric of Strasbourg; son of Jean Choltz and Marie Kairien; died 27 August 1738.

JOSEPH CHREYER - Swiss soldier; died 10 July 1757.

LEON SONT CIPERTZ - Native of the canton of Bade; buried 23 December 1742.

MARIANE GUILLETTE - Native of Belle Isle in Brittany.
    GABRIELLE - Baptized 20 August 1738; buried 9 November 1738.

JACOB CLAUSE - Native of Marpin in Lorraine, parish of St. Sepaslier, diocese of Treves; son of Jean Clause and Marguerite Chasseur; died 7 June 1743.
    (Note: Antoine Clause who was buried 20 November 1742, age thirteen months, is possibly his son.)

SIMON CLIMPELLE dit BONVIRAIN - Soldier in Bonille's company; died 21 October 1751.

JEAN COFMAN - Swiss soldier in Halleville's regiment; buried 23 April 1758.

CHARLES COLET - Swiss soldier in Karer's regiment; died 30 January 1749.

FRANCOIS COLIN - Died 4 April 1769, on his Tensa habitation.
    (Note: One Marie Francoise Colein died 22 December 1758; no relationship was indicated, however.)

JEAN COLON - Sergeant in de Chateauguay's company; habitant of Dauphine Island.
    MARGUERITE PRAU (PROT) (PREAU)
        JEAN - Born 4 November 1707.
        ISAAC - Born 18 September 1709.
        ANTOINE - Baptized 20 December 1712; died 6 November 1755; churchwarden.
        MARIE THERESE - Born 11 January 1715.
        MARIE MARGUERITE - Born 15 June 1717.
        MARIANNE PERINNE - Born 10 July 1722.

CHARLES COMPAGNON
    CATHERINE CHAGNEAU
        PIERRE CHARLES - Born 1 August 1721.

FRANCOIS COMPAGNOT - Soldier in Marchand's company.
    JEANNE LAFOND (LAFONT)
        DOMINIQUE FRANCOIS - Baptized 8 December 1726.
        ETIENNE - Born 1 June 1728.
        FRANCOIS - Baptized 15 December 1730, "<u>enfant naturel et legitime.</u>"
        JEAN RENE - Born 15 February 1733.

PIERRE CONDE - Native of Yagers in Galicia; "<u>forcat</u>" at Pensacola; buried 6 October 1744.

ANDRE CONNARD - Master wheelright.
    ELIZABETH THERESE BERNARD
        JEAN ANDRE - Baptized 12 October 1727.

JOSEPH CONTANT
    JEANNE MEGARD (?)
        MARIE LOUISE JOSEPHE - Baptized 28 September 1725.

JACQUES COQUELIN
    MARIE BOURGEOIS
        MARIE - Born 28 March 1720

PIERRE COSSORT
    MARIE LA FONTAINE LE PAGE
        (Son) - Born 20 March 1716.

SIMON COUSSOT - Master pilot for the king.
    MARTHE (MARIE) FLEIN (FLAYE)
        HYPPOLITE - Born 18 November 1710.
        PIERRE DANIEL - Born 22 September 1715.

JEAN CRESPEAU
    MARIE THERESE BROCHON
        MARIE JOSEPHE - Born 20 March 1719.

JEAN CROIX dit GRIMAULD - Habitant of Massacre Island.
    ANGELIQUE DROUIN (BROUIN)
        JEAN BAPTISTE - Born 8 February 1709.
        JACQUES - Born 20 December 1710.

PHILIPPE DANIAU
    ANNE THIBAUT
        MARIE ANNE - Born 3 May 1720.

MICHEL DANTY
    JEANNE CHATELLIER
        MARIE MARGUERITE - Born 7 September (1720).

PIERRE DANTY - Habitant of Massacre Island.
    MARIE CHATELIER
        MARIE THERESE - Born 28 October 1721.

ANTOINE BENOIST D'AQUIN - Officer of the garrison at Fort Condé.
    JEANNE RENEE GARNIER - Died 14 November 1733.
        MARGUERITE - Born 7 September 1727.
        ANTOINE PIERRE - Born 13 January 1729.
        ANTOINE FRANCOIS - Born 9 February 1730.

D'ARBANNE
    (D'Arbanne's Indian Slave)
        JEAN BAPTISTE - Baptized 26 July 1710, about 6 months old.

GILBERT D'ARDENNE - Habitant of Fort Louis.
    MARGUERITE BUREL
        JEANNE - Born 2 April 1710.

DAUTERIVE - Chevalier de St. Louis; major at New Orleans; died before 18 December 1745.
    CHARLOTTE BOSSUA

BERTRAND JOSEPH DE BOISSY - "Enseigne-en-pied"; died 14 March 1755.

DE BONNILLE - "Ancien capitain" of the French troops; Chevalier de St. Louis; died 3 November 1767.

CREPIN DE CONTE - Seigneur de Pechon; ecuyer; major at Fort Toulouse des Alibamonts; infantry captain; died 29 February 1736, at Fort Toulouse, according to Michel Goudeau, surgeon and guardian of the warehouse at the fort.
    ANNE GENEVIEVE (CATHERINE) DE REMONT (REMOND)
        ANTOINE - Born 7 March 1723.
        MARIE LOUISE - Born 10 April 1725.
        BERNARD - Born 11 April 1729.

(Daughter) - Born 24 September 1730.
JOSEPH CREPIN - born 27 February 1733; buried 9 March 1733.
AUGUSTIN CREPIN - Born 11 January 1734.

FRANCOIS DECORSE - Sailor; died 14 December 1753.

CHARLE FRANCOIS DE CREMONT - Commissioner of the Marine and judge at Fort Condé.
URSULE DE MOLONDRON
ANNE DE CREMONT
    CHARLE MATHIAS - Born 2 December 1732; buried 28 December 1732.

PIERRE NICOLAS ANNIBAL DE VELLE - Captain of a detached company of the Marine.
CONSTANCE DE LUSSER
    (Daughter) - Born 7 February 1742; buried 7 February 1742.
    MARIE MARGUERITE - Buried 1 July 1747, 6 months old.

JEAN DEFFIN - Soldier of the 34th company; buried 26 August 1754.

LOUIS DE FLANDRE - "Greffier" and notary at Fort Condé; (Note: One record of a child's baptism indicates that he was a native of La Motte; his funeral record states: "native of Corbie, bishopric of Amiens in Picardy."); died 26 April 1748.
MARIE THERESE DU PRE
    JEAN BAPTISTE - Baptized 30 September 1731.
    LOUIS - Born 9 October 1733.
    JEAN PAUL - Born 19 March 1737.
    JEAN - Born 12 January 1739.
    (Note: One Jean de Flandre, age about 16 years, was buried 16 October 1757; no relationship is given.)

DE JUSAND - Officer of the militia.
    GABRIELLE GRANDVAL - Died 11 December 1754.

JEAN JOSEPH DE LA BESGE - Infantry officer; died 23 July 1745.

DE LA LANDE - Guardian of the king's storehouse.
    MARIE ANNE CHAUVIN - Died 4 December 1732.

CHARLES DE LA LANDE
    CHARLOTTE DUVALLE
        (Son) - Born 10 September 1738; Buried 10 November 1738.

PIERRE DE LANGE dit LA PLUME - Native of Bout de la Reine; soldier; buried 6 January 1742.

BARTHELEMY JUSTIN DE LA MARE - Lieutenant in the militia; "marchand-epicier" in Parish, on the corner of "Rue neuve St. Martin;" native of St. Nicholas des Champs parish; died 26 July 1738, of a "most violent pleuresy," when he was 48 years old.
    FRANCOISE DE VAUDEZARE - Native of Paris.

JEAN FRANCOIS DE LA PLACE dit MONTFORT - Sergeant in Le Sueur's company; native of Gisor in Normandy, diocese of Rouën; buried 8 April 1744.

NICOLAS DE LA SALLE - Acting Commissioner (As noted on records in 1708-1709.)
    JEANNE CATHERINE DE BERANHARD
        SIMON - Husband of Anne Petit.
        HENRY - Born 22 March 1708.
        MARIE - Born 24 August 1709; died 30 August 1709.

JOSEPH DE LAZON - Captain of the king's ship Aigle Noir; buried 22 September 1733.
    MARIE LOUISE BALIVET - Native of Chartres in Beauce; buried 20 April 1736.

JOSEPH DE LERY - Merchant at Fort Louis.
    HIPPOLITE MERI
        JOSEPH - Born 5 October 1709.

JEAN DE LOBELLE - Died 23 October 1745.

JEAN DELOTS dit MOUSTACHE - Invalid, from a place two "lieux" from Bayonne, diocese of Lescar; buried 11 October 1737.

HENRY DE LOUBOEY - Chevalier de St. Louis; "ancien capitain" of Navarre; Commandant at Biloxi and Fort Condé de la Mobile; died 7 September 1749.
    MARIE MODHUI (?) DE ST. SIMON
        MARIE ANNE - Baptized 23 November 1725.

FRANCOIS CLAUDE DELPHIE - Swiss soldier in Karrer's regiment; died 19 September 1749.

JOSEPH CHRISTOPHE DE LUSSER - Ecuyer; Seigneur d'Abek; officer in the Louisiana troops and aide-major at Mobile in 1724.
    MARGUERITE DE BOURASSE
        MARGUERITE CONSTANCE - Born 10 September 1720.
        MARIE JOSEPH - Born 13 February 1722.
        (Son) - Baptized 4 April 1724.
        LOUIS FRANCOIS - Born 5 January 1726.
        JEAN BAPTISTE JOSEPH - Born 4 June 1735.

JEAN CHARLES DE MOUY - Habitant and captain of militia; buried 3 November 1758.

JEAN CHARLES DE MOUY - Died 8 November 1752.
    MARIE JOSEPHE ROCHON
        JEAN CHARLES - Buried 1742.

NICOLAS DE MUSTEL dit FRANC COEUR
    MARIANNE MANSEAU - Died 19 January 1757.

LOUIS DENIS - Eccuyer, Sieur de Bonnaventure.
    FRANCOISE LE FEBVRE
        FRANCOISE CLAUDINE - Born 23 March 1720.

NOEL DE PROUEN (PRONOUD) - Habitant of Mobile River.
    LOUISE VALDE (WALTE) (VUALDRE) (DE VALLEE) (WALTRE)
        MARIE JEANNE - Born 10 January 1722.
        ETIENNE NOEL - Born 24 December 1726.
        MARIE - Born 4 April 1729; died 19 May 1735.
        CATHERINE - Baptized 2 April 1731.
        MARIE LOUISE - Born 23 January 1734.

JEAN BAPTISTE DE ROY - Received abjuration from heresy 23 December 1722.

LOUIS DE ST. MICHEL - Of St. Germain en Laye; guardian of the storehouse for the Company of the Indies at the Balise; Buried 1 June 1732.

JEAN DESBERGE dit STE. CROIX - Soldier in Le Sueur's company; Buried 10 May 1739.
    MADELAINE BAUDOUIN

ANNE FRANCOISE - Born 10 August 1721.
PIERRE - Born 21 February 1725.

NICOLAS DESESART - Sailor on the Providence; buried 6 November 1739.

FRANCOIS DESLANDES - Buried 13 July 1733.
MAGDELAINE BOYER
HELENE - Born 2 November 1729.
FRANCOIS - Born 2 November 1729.
MARIE JEANNE - Born 8 May 1732.

SILVAIN DES MAISONS dit TOUT-LUY-FAUT - Soldier in Le Sueur's company; son of Jean Baptiste des Maisons and Marguerite Jubin; native of parish of St. Saturnin.

PIERRE DESORGES dit ST. JACQUES - Drowned 14 October 1741 at "Appalaches" with his wife. Their bodies were found two months later.
MARGUERITE ST. LAZARE - Drowned at "Appalaches" 14 October 1741.
JEANNE MARGUERITE - Born 5 May 1720.
PIERRE - Born 1 March 1725.
MARGUERITE - Born 31 January 1727.
JULIENNE - Born 3 March 1730.

PIERRE DEUX FACES dit LA FOND - Buried 3 October 1767.

JOSEPH DE VEAUX dit ST. AMAND - Soldier; son of Jean De Veaux and Marie Anne Preche; buried 17 August 1742.

JEAN DEVEKY - Soldier in the Fourth Swiss Company; native of Zurich, Switzerland; buried 14 December 1758.

VALENTIN DEVIN - Engineer at Fort Condé; buried 23 June 1735.
MARTHE CHAUVIN
(Son) - Buried 22 September 1732, ten days old.
VALENTIN - Born 10 March 1734.
MARIE MARTHE - Born 8 January 1736.

JEAN GREGOIRE DE VOLANT - Captain of a Swiss company.
MARTHE CHAUVIN
MARTHE CHARLOTTE - Born 22 June 1738.

ISAAC DIDIER

MARIE LA (DES) FONTAINE
    MARIE - Born 26 September 1717.
    ISAAC - Born 15 February 1720.

PETER DIK - Native of Switzerland; buried 13 September 1733.

PIERRE DOMAILLE - Died 18 December 1747.
JEANNE LA FOND - Buried 1 April 1747.

BLAISE DONOT dit LA FONTAINE - Of Nogent-sur-Seine.
MARIE FASINOT
    EDME - Buried on the seashore at the mouth of Fish River where he was found dead 16 September 1726.

MARTIN DOREE dit LEVEILLE - Soldier in Marchand's company; soldier in De Merveilleux's company; buried 14 December 1737.
JEANNE VALOIS (VALLON) (VALONE) (VALON) (VALENE) (VALLONE) - Died 27 September 1740; native of La Rochelle, parish of Notre Dame. (See ROBERT OLLIVIER)
    MARIE LOUISE - Born 18 June 1726; buried 20 June 1726.
    MARTIN - Born 8 November 1727.
    ("Fille naturel et legitime") - Born 8 December 1728.
    ANNE ROSE - Born 17 February 1731.
    MARIE JEANNE - Born 31 July 1732.
    MAURICE - Baptized 20 April 1735.
    URSULE - Baptized 1737; Buried 21 October 1739.

LOUIS DOSSEMAN
ANDREE ROBERTE GUILLET
    LOUIS PIERRE - Born 29 June 1719.

ZACHARIE DRAPEAU - Habitant of Fort Louis.
MARIANNE PREAU
    ANTOINE - Born 14 February 1717.
    ANNE - Born March 1719.
    JEAN - Born 17 October 1720.

HENRY DRISCOLLE - Merchant; died 6 November 1766.

BARTHELEMY DUBIC - Recouvreur.
ANNE GALBRUN
    ("Fille naturel et Legitime") - Born 4 December 1728.

FRANCOIS DUBOIS - Carpenter; buried 14 September 1761.

JEAN PIERRE DUBOIS
LOUISE VALDRE
    ANTOINE - Born 30 November 1738.

PIERRE DU BOIS - Swiss soldier; native of Gauvez, duchy of Savoy, bishopric of Chambery; buried 25 April 1757, 42 years old.

ESTIENNE DUBORDIEU - Notary and greffier at Fort Condé; buried 29 July 1735.

MICHEL DU BORDIEU - Ecuyer, Sieur de Hullot; married 28 August 1724.
    JEANNE KEROUEST - Widow of Sieur Le Compte, shipbuilder.

GUILLAUME DUCHESNE - Native of Cancasse, bishopric of St. Malo; buried 6 January 1741.

ETIENNE DU MECHE dit RAMEE - Soldier in Hazur's company; died 9 January 1750.

HUBERT DUMOIRU
JEANNE ELIZABETH BOISSINOT
    JEAN HUBERT - Baptized 23 January 1738; buried 25 January 1738.

JEAN NICOLAS AUBERT DUMONT - Died as the result of an accident at his Tensas habitation 17 April 1758.

CLAUDE DUPONT dit FRANCOEUR - Soldier in Marantin's company; son of Pierre Dupont and Marie Jeanne Vairet; native of Paris, parish of St. Gervais; died 30 November 1755, 39 years old.

JACQUES CLAUDE DU PONT - Native of Paris; soldier in the companies of La Tour, De Lusser, and Bertel; buried 3 April 1737.
    MARIANNE FOUCAUT - Native of Paris.
        CLAUDE - Born 9 February 1723.
        LAMBERT - Baptized 12 January 1727; died 25 October 1747. (See Pierre Galand)
        MARIE MAGDELAINE - Born 17 April 1729; died 25 October 1747. (See Pierre Galand)

PHILLIPPE - Born 15 November 1732;)
    died 8 October 1734.)
CATHERINE - Born 15 November 1732;) Twins
    buried 29 May 1733.)
(Son) - Born 9 January 1735.

JEAN DU PU----
    MARIE DU VAU
        JEAN - Born 9 January 1716.

CHARLE DUPUISSIEUX - <u>Ecrivain</u> at the Mobile office; buried 13 December 1757.

FRANCOIS DU PRE (DUPRET) - Bourgeois of Fort Louis; deceased by 16 February 1722
    MARIE MAGDELAINE OUANET
        MARIE THERESE - Born 15 October 1708.
        FRANCOIS - Born 18 December 1716.
        JEANNE MAGDELAINE - Born 11 December 1719.
        MARIE CHARLOTTE - Born 16 February 1722.

JACQUE DUPRE dit D'ARBONNE - Canadian; habitant of Mobile Bay; native of Montreal, habitant of Riviere aux Poules.
    ANNE MARIE BIENVENUE - Native of the parish of Plemier, bishopric of Renne in Brittany.
        ANNE - Born 4 January 1734.
        JEAN JACQUES - Born 3 April 1736.
        ELIZABETH - Born 10 June 1738.

JACQUE VINCENT DUPRE - Captain of a "<u>batiment marchand.</u>"
    MARIE THERESE BOUCHE - Native of Canada; buried 18 November 1743.

MAURICE DURAND - Died 13 December 1769.

JEAN DUVAL dit ST. JEAN - Native of Dieppe; buried 27 September 1733.

GUILLAUME DUVAT - Swiss corporal in De Lusser's company. (This name should be BURAT.)
    MAGDELAINE ROGE
        JOSEPH GUILLAUME - Born 13 January 1731.

CHARLE EGRON dit LAMOTTE - Habitant of Pensacola, dependent of the Mobile parish.
    FRANCOISE - Indian.

MARIE MAGDELAINE - Baptized 20 April 1728, six
months old.

JEAN ESCHETIN - Swiss soldier; native of the canton of Lucerne; buried 14 October 1761.

JACQUE FABUS - Native of the parish of Armantiere, bishopric of Soisson; died 3 September 1741.

FRANCOIS FAVRE - Turner; died 19 May 1756.

JEAN FAVRE (FABVRE)
MARIANNE D'ARLEU
JEAN SIMON - Born 28 October 1722.
(Infant Son) - Baptized 1725.

JEAN BAPTISTE FAVRE - Died 15 March 1725.

VALENTIN FEIFFVER - Soldier in a Swiss company; native of Spire in Germany; surgeon; buried 20 June 1759.

JOSEPH FICHET dit LA FORGE - Son of Marin Fichet and Charlotte La Jaine; native of Versailles, parish of Notre Dame; soldier in Hazur's company; died 15 September 1750.

ETIENNE FIEVRE - Master carpenter; buried 30 July 1760.
MARIE ANNE GRISE (GRISSE) - Died 12 June 1767.
(Daughter) - Baptized 3 April 1725.
ETIENNE VALENTIN - Born 13 October 1727.
FRANCOIS - Born 26 February 1730.
JEAN - Born 3 November 1733; buried 17 August 1736.
LOUIS - Born 8 January 1735; buried 29 October 1737.
(Note: One Jacque Fievre died 28 January 1767.)

JACQUES FINEAU - Died 8 March 1725, about 40 years old.
JEANNE DE LA FOND (FONT) (FOLLE)
MARIE JEANNE - Born 1 December 1717.
JEANNE - Born 24 January 1721; died 24 June 1749.
LOUISE MARGUERITE - Born 3 December 1722.
PIERRE - Baptized 4 June 1724; buried 6 March 1760.

THOMAS FITZGERALD - Irishman; died 19 July 1766.

LOUIS FLANDRIN - Died 10 February 1764.

JEAN FONTAIL (FONTAYE) - Soldier of De Mandeville's company; married 28 May 1724.
    MARIE LE MIR - Widow of Drapeau (?).
        (Daughter) - Baptized 22 September 1724.
        JEAN CHARLE - Baptized 12 December 1728, "<u>fils naturel et legitime</u>;" buried 9 June 1736.

LOUIS FONTENOT dit COLIN - Son of Joachim Fontenot and Jeanne Prido; native of Poitiers, parish of St. Germain; sergeant in De La Tour's company; sergeant in Merveilleux's company; married 8 February 1726.
    LOUISE HENRY - Daughter of Mathurin Henry and Louise de Perigo; native of Port Louis, parish of Blauet (Blavet ?); widow of La Bogne (?).
        PHILIPPE - Born 21 August 1727. (Note: On this record the mother is listed as Louise Perigot.)
        JEAN - Born 1 January 1729, "<u>fils naturel et legitime</u>.' (Note: On this record the mother is listed as Louise Perigot.)
        JEAN LOUIS - Born 27 February 1730. (Note: On this record the mother is listed as Louise Henry.)
    (Note: One Francois Fontenot, creole and soldier at Allibamons, was buried 16 January 1759.)

HERMAND FOUKCE - Son of Hermand Foukce and Anne Barbe; native of Luxembourg, parish of St. Nicolas; solier of the convoy of Tombecbe; drowned in Tombigbee River in August, 1742.

LOUIS FOURNIER - Native of Resnes in Brittany, parish of St. Francois. He came to the colony on the <u>Providence</u>, under command of Mr. de la Rodinier and Sieur Tiasset in 1739. Died 2 November 1740, fifteen years old.

PIERRE FOURNIER dit VINAREST - Soldier in Bonille's company; died 18 September 1752.

JOSEPH ANTOINE FRANC - Soldier in Vilmont's company; buried 27 September 1754.

JEAN BAPTISTE FREDERIC - Baron de Hombourg; <u>lieutenant reformé</u>; died 15 March 1744.

GEDEON FREMY
    ELIZABETH FARCOIS (sic)
        FRANCOIS - Born 24 August 1717.

JOSEPH SIMON FRISQUET - Surgeon; died 29 November 1744.

PIERRE GABRIEL dit MONTELIMAR - Native of Montelimar, bishopric of Valence in Dauphiné.
    MARIE ISABELLE LAMY - Native of Port Louis, diocese of Nantes in Brittany.
    MARIE JEANNE - Born 11 July 1737; buried 22 October 1739.

PIERRE GLAND dit LA CHAUMETTE - Native of Grandcé de Medary, parish of St. Gervais de Lé in Normandy; soldier in Bombel's company; massacred 23 October 1747, by the Choctaw Indians at his habitation, with his wife, his daughter, Marie Magdelaine Dupont, one named Lambert du Pont, Pierre Mozel, and a Negress named Agatte, who belonged to Mozel. They were buried 25 October 1747.
    MARIE ANNE FOUCAULD - Native of St. Eustache, parish of Paris.
    MARIE JEANNE - Born 26 December 1736.

JEAN BAPTISTE GALANT - Master canoneer; native of Rochefort in Xaintonge; buried 12 December 1736.

JOSEPH GARDON - Chartier; soldier in De Merveilleux's company.
    MARIE JEANNE TABOURET - Sage femme of Fort Condé; buried 29 November 1735.
    HELENE - Born 15 February 1728.
    JEAN JOSEPH - Born 29 April 1730.

JOSEPH GARDON dit LA JEUNESSE - Steward for Mr. La Lande; native of Poitevin, parish of St. Porchere; buried 13 December 1740.
    JEANNE ANGELIQUE LAYIE - Native of Guadeloupe, parish of St. Francois; daughter of Nicolas Laye and Angelique Froyer; died 11 June 1743.
    CHARLOTTE - Born 15 June 1738.

ETIENNE DENIS GASQUET dit MONTOUE - Soldier; native of Paris, parish of St. Nicolas des Champs; died 30 October 1748.

ETIENNE GERBIER - Soldier; native of Bourges; died 15 May 1755, 26 years old.

ETIENNE GERMAIN dit LONGEDOC - Soldier in Hazur's company; died 16 April 1751.

LOUIS GILBERT - Native of Tremblade, diocese of Xaintes in Xaintonge; buried 17 February 1738.

JEAN GIRARD - Patron for the King; native of the city and diocese of Renne in Brittany, parish of St. Aubin; buried 15 November 1758.
    MARIE ANNE DANIAU - Creole of Mobile; died 7 September 1754.
    MARIE JEANNE - Baptized 29 June 1737.

PIERRE GIRARD dit LANGOUVRAY - Soldier; buried 5 November 1757.

GEORGE GOUPPY - Native of Muzante, diocese of Mans; French soldier; buried 6 August 1760.

JACQUES ALEXANDRE GRENAT - Soldier; son of Pierre Grenat and Marguerite Rousseau; native of St. Laurent parish, Paris; buried 15 October 1736.

FRANCOIS GRIGNON dit BELLE ETOILE - Soldier in De Lusser's company; buried 5 Nune 1736.

NICOLAS GUE - Soldier of the garrison at Fort Louis
    JEANNE VERGNE
        MARIE ANNE - Born 7 October 1718.
        FRANCOIS - Born 13 October 1720.
        PIERRE NICOLAS - Born 3 September 1722.

LOUIS JEAN GUERIN - Botanist; native of Paris; buried 18 October 1737.

GUETELIN
    CATHERINE VOLANT - buried 22 August 1762.

GREGOIRE GUILLORY - Habitant of Fish River.
    MARIE JEANNE LA CASE - Died 27 April 1764.
        LOUISE - Died 2 May 1749, 10 months old. Her father declared that she died in his absence and that only his wife and an old man named Dauphin were there and had to bury her because they could not carry the body to the fort.

SIMON HABIBIN - Native of Recouvrance, Brest, in Brittany; sailor on the Aigle Noir, and carpenter; buried 11 September 1733.

PIERRE HALIN
    MARIE PHILIPPE - Native of Maux in Brie; buried 13
    March 1726.

FRANCOIS HAMON DE COURCHAN - Pilot and captain.
    MARGUERITE COLON
        FRANCOIS - Born 15 May 1734.

JEAN HARLU - Master builder.
    CATHERINE BASILE
        MARIE CATHERINE - Born 31 December 1719.

HAZUR
    (WIFE NOT LISTED)
        JEAN FRANCOIS - Died 22 February 1749, 5 years
            and 8 days old.
        JOSEPH CHRISTOPHLE - Died 27 February 1749,
            about 4 years old.
        CATHERINE PELAGIE - Died 5 November 1749,
            about 8 months old.

ANTOINE HENRY - Sergeant in Sorenne's company; died 13
December 1756.

ROBERT HELIE - Native of St. Lot, bishopric of Constance;
buried 3 September 1734.

JEAN HERO (HERAUT) - Master joiner.
    MARIE REAL (REINNE)
        JEAN JACQUES - Born 22 September 1721.
        JEAN BAPTISTE - Baptized 24 August 1725.

JOSEPH HERTEL DE ROUVILLE - Ensign in the troops; died
18 September 1743.

FRANCOIS HERTHEY dit PAQUIER
    MAGDELAINE BOYER
        IGNACE FRANCOIS - Born 16 April 1726

JEAN HERTZINAN - Swiss soldier.
    MARIE UTSIGER - Native of Baldingen, jurisdiction of
    Baden; buried 22 September 1757.

JEAN BAPTISTE HERVIEUX - Native of Quebec; master
arquebusier; married 18 September 1724.
    ANNE (MARIE) PEAUX (PRAUX) - Widow of Hussot.

JEAN BAPTISTE - Born 11 July 1726.
JEANNE - Born 16 March 1728.

JEAN PIERRE HINGLE - Carpenter; died 11 January 1766.

JEAN BAPTISTE HOUSET dit LA LOIRE
   MARIE ANNE NADEOUT
      LOUISE - Born 23 February 1707.

MARC ANTOINE HUBERT - Ecquier; commissaire-ordonnateur.
   ELIZABETH CESTERI
      (Male Infant) - Born 18 May 1718.

MARC ANTOINE HUCHE - Interpreter for the King.
   THERESE COLON
      MARIE THERESE HENRIETTE - Born 28 January 1732; buried 20 July 1732.
      MARC ANTOINE - Born 18 December 1733.

MARC ANTOINE HUCHE
   MAURICETTE QUERVEGAN
      MARIE THERESE - Born 17 March 1716.
      MARIE ANNE - Born 22 January 1719.

HUET
   PERINNE ROETTE - Died 27 November 1767.

EDWARD HURCKSALL - Native of Citimboure, province of Kent, England; 8 September 1727, renounced the heresy of Protestantism and accepted the Roman Catholic faith.

CLAUDE HUSSON dit VAUCOULEUR - Soldier in Le Sueur's company; died 12 May 1750.

BARTHELEMY HUVIC - master coverer.
   ANNE JALBREN
      MARIE LOUISE - Born 31 May 1726.

PIERRE INNERICK - Soldier in Marrer's company; native of Treves; died 20 September 1751.

CHRISTIAN INSLIN - Swiss soldier in Grondel's company; died 5 January 1754, after having made abjuration from Lutherism.

JEAN JADARD DE BEAUCHAMPS - Chevalier de St. Louis; lieutenant of the king and commandant of the "Department de Mobile;" buried 23 October 1754.
    MARIE LE SUEUR - Buried 10 March 1755
    (Note: Among witnesses was Monsieur de Kerlerec,
        Chevalier de St. Louis, captain of the king's vessels, and governor of the province.)

RENE JALOT
    MARIE DE LOUMEAU
        MARIE CATHERINE - Born 9 March 1720.

RENE JAMBE - Soldier in the Fourth Company of Hallwal's Swiss regiment; native of Beaufort in Savoy; buried 21 January 1758.

PIERRE JOSEPH JEAN - Solder in the Thirty-Fourth Company; buried 23 September 1754.

VINCENT JOLIN dit DUBRUILLE
    MARGUERITE VALTER
        LOUISE MARGUERITE - Died 30 May 1739, buried at their habitation at Bay Minette, due to the lack of a priest or consecrated ground.

JOSEPH - Bohemian; invalid.
    MARIE AGNES SIMON - Bohemian of Arbrist.

PIERRE JUSAN - Aide-major de la place.
    MARIE FRANCOISE TRUDOT - Buried 25 March 1736.
        PIERRE - Born 20 March 1736.

PHILIPE KLEINPETRE - Died 13 March 1766, at his habitation at Tensas, where he was buried.

VALENTIN KREDEL - Soldier in the Swiss regiment; native of Hausen in Briseau, Germany; died 3 March 1756, 35 years old.

KREPS
    MARIE JOSEPHE LA POINTE - Died 7 November 1751.
    MATHIAS - Died 18 September 1751, 4 years old.

LA BATERIE - Swiss; shoemaker; buried 1 July 1759.

JEAN LA CASE - Soldier in Marchand's company; died 21

June 1726.
    MARIANNE FOURCHE
        JEAN PIERRE - Born 19 January 1721.
        JACQUES - Born 23 September 1722.
        MARIE JEANNE - Born 20 March 1726.

GERMAIN LA FARGE
    (INDIAN) - Slave belonging to Marchand.
    LOUIS FRANCOIS - Baptized 4 December 1723.

MAURICE LA FONTAINE - Native of Versailles; soldier; buried 12 September 1734.

CHARLES LAGARDE - Died 23 June 1749.

LAIDEK - Tailor
    MARIE CATHERINE VALADE - Died 25 November 1754.

LA MARE
    CLAUDINE DE BEAUVOIS - Died 3 January 1748.

PIERRE LANGLOIS - Soldier; native of Tours in Tourraine; Buried 10 December 1757.

LAPPALU (?)
    MAGDELAINE ROBERT
        JEANNE - Born 1719.

JOSEPH LA PRADE - Buried 22 January 1759.

JEAN JORGES LARCH - Swiss soldier; native of Villiseaux, canton of Berne; buried 24 November 1754.

JEAN BAPTISTE LARDAZE - Surgeon; died 5 June 1764.

DURAND LA ROCHE
    MARIE VILAINE
        MARIE FRANCOISE - Born August 1719.

JACQUE LA ROCHE - Soldier; son of Joseph La Roche and Marguerite Elissé; native of Marate in Auvergne, bishopric of St. Flurs; buried 23 October 1737.

ESTIENNE LA TRONCHE
    OLIVE BOULY
        ESTIENNE ELISABETH - (Male) Baptized 9 Novem-

ber 1715.

LAURENT LAURENT - Soldier in De Merveilleux's company; soldier in De Lusser's company; buried 14 August 1737.
    JEANNE MAHOULD (MAHOU)
        JOSEPH - Born 2 January 1729, at Fort Toulouse.
        MARIE JEANNE - Born 16 January 1732; buried 30 April 1733.
        MARIE JEANNE - Born 22 January 1736.

PIERRE LA VALLEE - Master maker of edge-tools.
    MAGDELAINE ALEXANDRE
        PIERRE ROBERT - Born 3 April 1731.

PIERRE LAVIGNE - Soldier in De La Tour's company; soldier in De Lusser's company; buried 17 July 1746.
    MARIE HENRIETTE TIENSA (ESTIENNE) (TIEU) (KING) (TIENNE)
        PIERRE - Baptized 30 November 1726; buried 12 December 1726.
        PIERRE - Baptized 24 July 1728.
        JEAN BAPTISTE - Born 28 January 1731.
        (Son) - Buried 19 May 1733.
        MARIE - Born 18 December 1738; buried 23 December 1738.

MICHEL LAVINE dit LA BRIE - Smelter; soldier in De Velle's company; son of Antoine Lavine and Marie Collin; native of Lesigny in Brie, parish of St. Martin, diocese of Paris.

JEAN LE BAIL dit BARON - Native of Favost in Brittany, bishopric of Quimper; buried 22 December 1734, 27 years old.

RENE LE BOEUF
    MARGUERITE TANCA
        CLAUDE - Born 11 February 1713.

RENE LE BOEUF
    THERESE - Christian Indian slave of Mr. Diron.
        LOUISE MARGUERITE - Baptized 5 June 1733, "fille naturel".

SAUINIEN LE BRETON
    ELIZABETH BRET
        MARIE ELIZABETH - Born 29 January 1721.

CLAUDE LE BRUN - Died 20 January 1766.

LOUIS LE BRUN - Carpenter; native of Toulon; died 30 July 1768.

LAURENT LE CHEVEUX - Soldier in Abin's company; buried 27 August 1754.

JACQUES LE COMPTE
JEANNE QUIRIOLES
JACQUES - Born 14 August 1715.

JACQUES LE FLEAU - Bourgeois of Mobile.
JEANNE BOISSINOT - Died 11 August 1752.
MARIE LOUISE - Died 30 May 1749.
LOUIS - Died 11 December 1749.

HENRY LOUIS LEGAT dit LE BRETON - Son of Jean Legat and Gillette Le Cars; native of Kimpere, parish of Lapsat, province of Brittany; soldier in De Velle's company; died 1 November 1737.

LE GRAND
    HYACINTHE GALLION
        (Son) - Baptized 8 January 1726.

FRANCOIS LE MAY - Maker of powder.
    ANNE ROUSSEAU
        (Male Infant) - Born 22 August 1704; died 22 August 1704.
        FRANCOIS BERNARD - Born 7 March 1709.

MARTIN LE PRINCE - Native of the parish of Notre Dame at Versailles; cadet in De Bombel's company; buried 15 May 1734.

FRANCOIS LE ROUX - Sailor; carpenter; native of Musilliac, jurisdiction of Redon in Brittany; died 14 August 1751.

PIERRE LE ROY - Sailor for the Company.
    CLAUDINE VIVIER - Native of Contreban; died 22 July 1726.

JOSEPH ANDRE LESCOUBE dit ST ANDRE - Corporal in Hazur's company; died 6 February 1749.

JEAN PAUL LE SUEUR - Major of Mobile; Chevalier de St. Louis; died 13 October 1751.
    MARGUERITE MESSIER DE ST. MICHEL - Native of Canada; died 5 March 1741.

PIERRE LETELLIER - Turner.
    MARIE ANNE JOURNEE
        MARIE MARGUERITE - Born 25 February 1726.

JEAN BAPTISTE LE VASSEUR - Corporal in Membret's company; native of St. Eustache parish, Paris; buried 29 March 1736.

LINDUQUE (?) - Tailor; buried 6 May 1762.

LOISEL - Locksmith for the king.
    MARIE CATHERINE BACQUE - Buried 30 April 1736.
    (Son) - Buried 23 April 1736.

PIERRE PAUL LOISEL - Locksmith; died 5 December 1745.
    MARIE LEMIRE - Died 15 July 1743.
        ANGELIQUE CATHERINE - Baptized 2 December 1737.

JEAN BAPTISTE LOLIER dit LA DERIVE - Soldier at Massacre Island; son of Jean Baptiste Lolier and Catherine Lanar; native of Cassy, diocese of Paris; drowned in the lagon of Massacre Island. Reported by the officers and soldiers of the island on 24 November 1742.

PIERRE LORANDINE - Soldier in Marchand's company; corporal in De Lusser's company; died 18 August 1768.
    MARIE FRANCOISE or MARIE ANNE FOURCHET
        (Daughter) - Baptized 13 November 1725.
        MARIE LOUISE - Baptized 10 March 1732.
        JEAN BAPTISTE - Born 10 February 1736.

JEAN LORANSONT dit BEAULIEU
    JEANNE MARGUERITE HEUGER (EUGENE) (EUGER)
        CECILLE MARGUERITE - Born 19 January 1722.
        CATHERINE - Baptized 12 September 1723.
        JEANNE MARGUERITE - Born 5 January 1727.

JACQUES LORREIN
    MARIE AVRIL

PIERRE CHARLES - Born 29 June 1727.
MARIE PELAGIE - Born 13 April 1729.
FRANCOIS - Born 27 August 1734.

JACQUES LUCIEN - Died 26 March 1769.
MARIE COLPE - Native of Mobile; died 26 July 1757.

PIERRE LUCKE dit ST. EUSTACHE - Soldier in Le Sueur's company.
    CATHERINE FEGER
        MARIE CATHERINE - Born 28 December 1738.

FELIX LUVAT - Native of La Rochelle, parish of Saint Nicolas; drowned in the ance de Mandeville, 29 September 1738.
    MARIE THERESE CORHUEL (CORNUEL)
        MARIE THERESE - Born 7 December 1720.
        (Daughter) - Born 13 February 1725.

PIERRE MA----- (?)
    ELIZABETH GEORGE
        ANDRE - Born 8 January 1725.

PIERRE MAIGRE - Son of Sieur Maigre, marchand epicier at Heneuer; buried 27 September 1734.

CLAUDE CLOY MAISIER dit MONT BARREY - Soldier in De La Maziliere's company; died 23 April 1758.

NICOLAS MALET - Soldier in Benoit's company; native of Dijon; died 23 March 1736.

MICHEL MANDRE
    BARBE CANDRAGUE
        LOUISE CATHERINE - Born 2 April 1721.

MARCHAND - Ecuyer; native of Coursel; captain of a detached company of the Marine.
    (NO WIFE LISTED)
        FRANCOIS - Buried 27 May 1733, "fils naturel," 10 years old.

JEAN MARCHAND dit LA CROIX – Soldier.
    JEANNE POUILLOT
        (Infant Daughter) - Born 8 October 1721.

ANTOINE MARIE - Habitant of Mobile; son of Jean Baptiste

Marie, wine merchant, and Louise Piteau of Isle St. Louis in Paris; buried 8 November 1739.
JEANNE MARGUERITE DES ORGES - Native of Mobile.

ANTOINE MARIE - Native of Paris, parish of St. Nicholas du Chardonnet; married 13 January 1725.
JULIETTE GUILLAUME - Native of Hennebon, diocese of Vanne.

FRANCOIS MARTIN dit L'ESPERANCE - Soldier in Bonnille's company; son of Pierre Martin and Magdelaine Robert; native of Orleans, parish of St. Paterne; buried 21 July 1751.

HILAIRE MARTIN dit ST. HILAIRE DUGLACIS - Soldier; son of Francois Martin and René PRONTAIE; native of St. Florin; parish of St. Hilaire, diocese of Angers; died 18 July 1751.

THOMAS MARTIN dit ST. MARTIN - Soldier in Hazeur's company; native of St. Va-----, diocese of Rouen; son of Jean Martin and Charlotte Beauval; died 12 May 1751.

NICOLAS MAUGET dit ST. CLAUDE - Native of Versailles; soldier in Bertet's company; buried 19 November 1733.

CHRISTIAN MAYER - Native of Constain, province of Salbourg; soldier of a Swiss company in Karrer's regiment; died 12 September 1751.

JEAN MAYER - Native of Faigrechesne in Alsace, diocese of Strasbourg; died 30 December 1741.
JEANNE FINAUX - Died 22 December 1741.

CHARLES MAZURE - Native of St. Malo; contremaistre on the Providence; died 20 August 1739.

FRANCOIS GUILLAUME MELISAN - Master surgeon; died 3 December 1749, on the road to the Alibamons.
MARIE MAGDELAINE BOYER
MAGDELAINE - Born 7 August 1736.

JACQUES MELONY - Irishman; died 7 July 1764.

PONIE MEREAU
JEANNE BLAISE
MARIE ANNE - Born 7 June 1720.

CHARLES FRANCOIS MERIER
   MARIE SUZANNE LE MOINE
      MARIE CATHERINE - Born 18 November 1720; died 28 November 1720.

NICOLAS ANTOINE MESSEIN - Son of Toussaint Messin and Suzanne Vry; native of Metz, parish of St. Martin; died 8 June 1751.

HENRY JOSEPH MILON - Native of Rheims; carpenter; entrepreneur for the king; died 8 (?) January 1744.
   MARIANNE (MARIE FRANCOISE) GIRARDY - Creole of Louisiana.
      JACQUES - Born 3 November 1736.
      JEAN - Born 29 November 1738.

PIERRE ETIENNE MILON - Habitant; died 16 November 1744.

GILBERT MINARD - Sergeant; son of Claude Minard and Claudine Devau; native of Moulin in Bourbonnois; died 20 January 1754.

JEAN MINARD dit BEAULIEU
   CATHERINE ROCQUES (ROQUET)
      CATHERINE - Born 2 November 1719.
      ANNE - Born 3 September 1720; died 3 September 1720.
      LOUIS RENE - Born 9 February 1722.

MINGUINE - Soldier; buried 22 May 1759.

MINGUY - Swiss soldier; buried 5 October 1737.

JEAN LOUIS MINUIT - Master canoneer.
   JEANNE L'ECRUE
      JEAN HONORE - Born 18 June 1707.

ANDRE MIOT - Soldier in De Lusser's company; steward for Monsieur de la Lande; patron for the king; died 21 August 1757.
   MARIE ANGELIQUE GIRARD
      JEANNE ANGELIQUE - Born 5 April 1731.
      CHARLE - Born 5 March 1735.
      (Note: One JEANNE MION died 15 August 1748; no relationship to the above family was given.)

NICOLAS MIRADO (MIRAUDO) - Died 15 September 1725.
ANGELIQUE RUISO (ROSNO) (RENEE)
    JEANNE - Born October 1723   ) Twins
    ANGELIQUE CLAUDE - Born October 1723)
    LAURE ANTOINE - Baptized 13 September 1725.
    ANDRE (Female) - Baptized 13 September 1725.

BARTHELEMY MONCLIN - Negociant; died 9 May 1756.

GABRIEL MONTELIMART
MARIE ELIZABETH LAMIE - Died 8 May 1757, 55 years old.

JEAN BAPTISTE MONTENARI - Native of Parma, Italy.
MARGUERITE TALON
    JEAN BAPTISTE - Born 21 February 1738.

ANTOINE MOREAU - Sailor for the king; died 3 August 1757.

PIERRE MOSEL - German soldier in de la Tour's company; died 25 October 1747 (See Pierre Galand.)
MARIE LOUISE (ELIZABETH) GAULTRE (COTTER) (GOTTE) - Died 15 November 1742, at their habitation on the Tombigbee River.
    ANDRE - Buried 21 December 1726, 2 years old.
    CLAUDE - Born 20 October 1727.
    BERNARD - Born 23 September 1730.
    JEAN PIERRE - Born 25 April 1733.
    MARIE ELIZABETH - Buried 26 August 1739.

NICOLAS MUNIER
PERRINE LA MARRE
    MICHEL - Born 15 July 1715.

NICOLAS MUNIER - Native of Versailles.
ELIZABETH RUALLANT - Native of Pont Corp (?) in Brittany; died 16 March 1726.

PATRICE MURPHIIS - Irishman of Pensacola; died 6 November 1767.

LOUIS NICOLLE dit ST. LOUIS - Soldier in Hazeur's company; died 12 April 1751.

JEAN BAPTISTE NOLAN - Irishman; lieutenant in the De Bourg regiment; died 1 May 1726.

JACQUES OBRIAN - Irishman; died 16 April 1766.
(Note: One MARIE OBRIAN died 9 August 1766; no relationship with the above was given.)

ROBERT OLIVIER dit JOLIBOIS - Buried 5 September 1754.

ROBERT OLLIVIER dit JOLI BOIS
    JEANNE VALLONE - Native of La Rochelle, parish of Notre Dame; widow of Martin Doré; died 27 September 1740.

ROBERT OLLIVIER dit JOLI BOIS - Habitant of Massacre Island.
    MARIE ANNE DARNELLE - Native of the environs of La Rouchelle, diocese of Leucon; died 23 September 1739.

BONAVENTURE OUDOIN - Turner for the king; buried 2 July 1758.

PIERRE OUVE
    JULIENNE RICHARD - Native of Vanne in Brittany; died 14 February 1733.

LOUIS PAGOT - Soldier in De La Tour's company.
    JEANNE GALLOIS
        MARIE - Born 19 September 1721.

PAIOU - Aide-major of the garrison at Fort Louis.
    (HIS INDIAN SLAVE)
        OLIVE - Born 30 January 1715.

PIERRE PAQUET - Habitant of Mobile Bay.
    MAGDELEINE - Natural daughter of Baudraud dit Graveline.
        MARIE MARTHE - Born 4 May 1736.

FRANCOIS PARANT (PARENT) - Master tailor; master blacksmith.
    MARIANNE ARLU - Buried 27 October 1755.
        FRANCOIS - Born 17 September 1727.
        CLAUDE - Baptized 4 June 1729; buried 10 June 1736.
        FRANCOISE - Born 21 August 1730.
        CHARLE - Baptized 22 January 1738.

CLAUDE PARISI - Soldier in Vilmont's company; buried 8 September 1754.

JEAN PASSERET dit LA CHAISE - Soldier; native of Toulouse, parish of St. Etienne; buried 21 February 1755.

JEAN PATEFIELD
    (WIFE NOT NAMED) - Died 16 July 1766.

ANDRE PAU
    JEANNE LA FOND
        CATHERINE - Born 3 March 1719.

PIERRE PAULET - Soldier in De La Tour's company.
    MANON (MARIE ANNE) (MARGUERITE) GABRIOT (POTIER)
        ETIENNE - Baptized 2 -?- 1723; buried 10 April 1733.
        GUILLAUME - Born 16 June 1727.
        PIERRE JOACHIM - Born 30 December 1729; buried 26 April 1733.
        (Note: One ANTOINE PAULET, 2 years old, was buried 26 August 1757, and another by the same name, a habitant, on 27 December 1757.)

ANDRE PENIGAULT - Master carpenter.
    MARGUERITE CATHERINE PREVOST
        RENE ANDRE - Born 27 October 1708.
        JACQUE - Baptized 28 March 1710.

JEAN FRANCOIS PERROT - Sergeant in Lagotterais' company; son of Claude Etienne Perrot, procureur, and Jeanne Antoinette Bernard; native of Besancon, parish of Ste. Marie Magdelaine; buried 10 October 1755, 47 years old.

OLIVIER PHILIPPE - Native of the village of Ste. Marie in Flanders, diocese of Cambray; captain of militia; died 27 December 1748; married 1 May 1724.
    LOUISE MARGUERITE HUSSOT; niece of Dominique Belzaguy; native of Chaly, diocese of Tours (?), in Louvain.

OLIVIER PHILIPPE - Deceased before 3 June 1753.
    MARIE ELIZABETH LISLE - Died 3 June 1753.

FRANCOIS PHILIPPE DE MANDEVILLE - Chevalier de St. Louis and Captain-Commandant at Mobile. On 4 August 1722, the Superior Council ordered the priest, Father Amand, to enter in the church records that this family name is actually

PHILIPPE and that the above's full name is as entered here. The subject signed "Marigny Demandeville."

MADELAINE LE MAIRE
    ANTOINE - Born 17 July 1721.
    (Son) - Born 1 January 1724; died 1 January 1724.

NOEL PICARD - Son of Noel Picard and Nicolle Elizabet Garleau; native of Rouagnon, diocese of Rheims; buried 26 January 1742.
    MARIE FRANCOISE LAPLACE - Native of Sanspuis, diocese of Amiens in Picardy; buried 20 January 1742.

GERVAIS PIGEON dit ST. BRICE - Son of Jean Pigeon and Marie Livrant; native of St. Brice in Normandy, diocese of Aurange; soldier in Le Sueur's company; died 14 November 1749.

JEAN PILLOTE (PIRAUBE)
ANNE DENIS (?)
    MARIE LOUISE - Born 20 April 1720; died 28 June 1720.

URBAN PINHUIR - Buried November 1759.

CLAUDE PINSDE (PINSDEZ) dit BOULANAIS - Sergeant of the troops, company of Marchand; native of Boulogne-Sur-Mer; son of Claude Pincedet and Marguerite Boulogne; married 4 April 1725; buried 2 January 1738.
    MARGUERITE PRAU - Widow of La Violette; died 24 January 1749.
        CLAUDE - Born 9 March 1726.
        MARIE FRANCOISE - Born 15 February 1728.
        FRANCOIS - Born 8 July 1731; buried 28 February 1733.

THOMAS PLANCHETTE - Native of Dublin, Ireland; died 16 July 1764.

ETIENNE POIRIE - Sergeant-major at Mobile; buried 8 December 1759.
    MARIE FRANCOISE BRIGNAC - Buried 17 November 1758.

JOSEPH POIRIER - Merchant-peddlar of the island of Santo Domingo who came to Mobile on the Poule . . . avec les sentiments d'un bon chretien; buried 29 May 1738.

JOSEPH POUPART dit LA FLEUR - Died at Fort Toulouse 12 March 1739.
   MARIE ROY
      MARIE JOSEPH - Born 10 December 1731.
      BERNARD - Born 1 September 1733; buried 23 September 1738.
      CATHERINE - Baptized 8 January 1736.

MATHIEU PRARERE
   MARIE ANTOINETTE TALE DE ROBEC - Native of Vienna, Austria; buried 31 August 1733. (Note: "DE ROBEC" may indicate geographical location and not actually be a part of the name.)

ANTOINE PREVOST - Orfevre.
   JEANNE MAGINET
      CHARLES - Born 30 June 1720.
      CLAUDE - Baptized 3 January 1725.
      JEANNE - Born 27 July 1727.

JEAN PROST
   ANNE PEROT - Buried 29 August 1739; 74 years old.

LOUIS PROU - Native of St. Laurent parish, Paris; soldier in De Lusser's company at Alibamons Post; buried 1 May 1733.

NOEL PROVAND - Died 26 August 1736.

RACHELE
   JEANNE DES ORGES - Buried 10 October 1754.

JEREMIE RACINS - Swiss soldier.
   JEANNE MEUSUIER
      GREGOIRE - Born 20 October 1735.

JEAN BAPTISTE RAGUET - "Greffier-en-chef" of the Louisiana Superior Council.
   MARIE LARIEUX
      JEAN BAPTISTE ANTOINE - Born 11 November 1721.

JEAN RAISON - Soldier in De Lusser's company; native of Paris; son of Jean Raison, master wheelright of Paris, Parish of St. Croix; buried 17 October 1733.

PIERRE JACQUES REGHAUND - Soldier in La Tour's company; soldier in De Lusser's company.
    MARIANNE CHATELLIER - Native of La Croix St. Oinet in Picardy; buried 22 August 1733.
        MARIE BAPTISTE - Born 8 February 1723.
        PIERRE ANTOINE - Baptized 5 January 1727.
        JACQUES LORENT - Born 4 May 1728.
        SUSANNE - Born 26 January 1730.
        JACQUES - Born 16 April 1732.

FRANCOIS RENAULD
    ANNE CHEVY
        THERESE - Natural daughter; born 2 April 1726.

PIERRE RENAULD
    (AN INDIAN SLAVE)
        JEAN BAPTISTE - Baptiste - Baptized 21 April 1728, 7 months old.

CHARLES REQUIEM - Native of the parish of St. Hilaire de la Celle of Poitier; soldier in Le Sueur's company; died 18 January 1750, on the road to the Alibamons.
    TOINETTE EULIE - Native of St. Paul parish in Paris.
        ANTOINE - Native of Mobile; buried 28 October 1757.
        MARIE JEANNE - Born at the Alibamons, 21 March 1731.
        (Note: One Michel Requiem died 9 July 1763. One Angelique Requiem, wife of Duplanti, died 16 February 1764.)

PIERRE LOUIS RETS - Native of Lesceille; soldier in Somme's company; buried 5 January 1763.

FRANCOIS RILLIEUX - Habitant of Pascagoula.
    MARIE RENEE ALEXANDRE (CHENET) (SENCHE)
        MARIE ANNE - Born 17 August 1732; her grandmother is Marie Anne Praux.
        MARGUERITE - Born 2 June 1734.
        JEANNE - Baptized 20 April 1738.

ANTOINE RIVARD
    MARIE BRUYARD
        GABRIELLE - Born 4 August 1707.
        MARIE GENEVIEVE - Born 8 December 1708.

PIERRE ROBERT

MARIANNE SARRASIN
    MARGUERITE - Born 29 August 1720; died 22 September 1720.

JEAN ROCHE - Buried 9 March 1767.

CHARLES ROCHON - Buried 22 March 1733.
    HENRIETTE COLON - Died 28 February 1733.
        CHARLES - Born 5 January 1716; buried 24 December 1747.
        PIERRE - Born 4 October 1717.
        MARIE HENRIETTE - Born 17 February 1720.
        MARIE JOSEPHE - Born 19 April 1722.
        LOUIS AUGUSTE - Baptized 14 May 1724.
        MARIE THERESE - Born 7 March 1726; buried 19 March 1733.
        JEAN - Born 25 December 1728, <u>fils naturel et legitime</u>; buried 8 February 1764.
        MARGUERITE - Born 21 April 1731.
        OLIVIER - Born 28 February 1733; buried 9 March 1733.

ALEXANDER ROGER dit BOUCHEFINE - Soldier in Grandchamp's company; died 22 November 1751.

LOUIS ROI
    (NO WIFE LISTED)
        PIERRE LOUIS - Born 21 December 1720.

NICOLAS ROI dit DAUPHIN - Buried 9 December 1759.

JEAN ROMAGONT - Habitant; locksmith; buried 19 December 1760.
    (Note: One Genevieve Romagont was buried 2 April 1761.)

FRANCISCO ROMANO - Native of Siviane, Spain; died 24 November 1766.

FRANCOIS RONDELON dit LA VALLE - Soldier in Welde's company; native of Argentre du Maine, diocese of Mans; son of Jean Claude Rondelon and Magdelaine Bonsar; 33 years old; buried 30 September 1738.

JEAN BAPTISTE ROUCEVE
    MARIE THERESE COLON
        JEAN FRANCOIS - Born 11 November 1737; died

4 October 1740; buried by his godparents in the absence of the priest.
PIERRE BERTRAND - Died 9 February 1749, about 4 years old.
JEAN BAPTISTE - Died 14 August 1754, 11 years old.

ALLAIN ROUSSEAU
   MARIE PHILIPPE
      MARIE ALLAIN ROUSSEAU - Baptized 30 August 1709.

NICOLAS ROUSSEAU - Habitant of Dauphine Island; native of Montereau Fautyone.
   CATHERINE NOTA (NAULA) - Native of Bayonne.
      CATHERINE - Born 24 March 1734.
      JEAN NICOLAS - Born 6 June 1736.

PIERRE ALLEIN ROUSSELIE - Native of Vanne in Brittany; buried 8 February 1738.

JACQUE ROY
   CATHERINE LUVAT - Died 13 September 1752.

JEAN ROY - Master canoneer.
   RENEE GUILBERT (GILBERT)
      JACQUE - Born 16 August 1705.
      JEAN PHILIPPE - Born 24 April 1708, at Massacre Island; died 1 October 1740.

LOUIS JACQUES ROY
   MARIE TURPIN
      PIERRE - Born 30 March 1726.

PIERRE ROY
   FRANCOISE MARTIN
      JEAN BAPTISTE - Buried 21 March 1737.

PIERRE ROY - Soldier in Merveilleux's company.
   FRANCOIS LA BROSSE (LA BRAU) (LA BREAU) - Buried 28 December 1745.
      JEAN - Born 12 November 1727.
      FRANCOISE - 25 March 1729.

SABOURDIN
   ANNE LANGE - Widow of Francois Hupé; died 28 No-

vember 1741.

RENE SABOURDIN
MARIE CLOTILDE JOUSO (FOUIOT)
MATHIEU - Baptized 23 April 1725.
MARIE FRANCOISE - Baptized 9 June 1726.

LOUIS SAILLIER
THERESE BRETT
(Son: LOUIS ?) - Born 11 February 1730.

BLAISE ST. MARTIN - Shoemaker; native of Aix in Provence; son of Etienne St. Martin and Marie Aubanel; buried 23 June 1743.

JEAN SANSOT dit DE LA GRANGE - Corporal in La Tour's company.
GABRIELLE SAVARY
JEANNE GABRIELLE - Born 18 October 1721.

JEAN SAUCIER (?)
MARGUERITE ARLU
(Daughter) - Baptized 11 November 1725.

JEAN BAPTISTE SAUCIER - Merchant at Fort Louis
GABRIELLE SAVARY
JEAN BAPTISTE - Born 27 November 1707.
JACQUES - Born 28 April 1710.

JEAN SCHMIDT - Swiss soldier of the Third Company of Karrer; died 20 December 1747.

JOSEPH SCHNIDER - Swiss soldier; native of Bretten in the Black Forest; buried 28 July 1754.

JEAN GEORGES SCHUCK - Native of Augsbourg; Swiss soldier; buried 28 September 1754.

JOSEPH SIMON dit LA POINTE
CATHERINE DOUSSIN - Died 30 March 1752.
(Note: One Marie Jeanne LaPointe, Madame Rochon, died 3 February 1764. One Jeanne La Pointe died 18 March 1764.)

JACOB SPRINGER - Swiss soldier in Karer's company; native of St. Viveillier, bishopric of St. Piser; died 4 August 1745.

JOSEPH STAMAIER dit CHATEAUNEUF - Soldier in Le Sueur's company; native of Dedaim in Artois, parish of Notre Dame, diocese of St. Homer; son of Joseph Stamier and Catherine Blanchard; died 1 September 1738.
    MARIE JEANNE LA CASSE

FREDERICK STAPPE - Shoemaker; died 17 January 1767.
    CHRISTINE ECRIVAIN - Died 10 September 1768.

JEAN STRAUS - Soldier in Karrer's company; died 29 August 1750.

AUGUSTIN STRONGK - Son of George Strongk and Marie Aulin; native of Scelestat, parish of St. Hubert, diocese of Strasbourg; sergeant of a Swiss company; drowned 26 March 1738.

GUILLAUME SULIVAN - Irishman; died 28 June 1766.

JEAN ROBERT TALENT - Died 5 August 1756, 17 years old.

ROBERT TALON - "First creole in this colony;" died 23 May 1745.

ROBERT TALON - Master joiner; master cabinetmaker.
(Note: One ROBERT TALON, Creole of Mobile, was buried 8 August 1746.)
    JEANNE PROT (PRAUX)
        JEANNE - Born 5 January 1719.
        MARGUERITE - Born 3 October 1721.
        JEAN BAPTISTE - Baptized 1 February 1726.
        HELENE - Born 9 September 1727; buried 7 May 1736.
        JEANNE - Born 6 April 1729; buried 10 May 1736.
        ANNE JEANNE - Born 27 February 1732; buried 13 May 1736.
        ANTOINE - Born 20 March 1734; buried 14 April 1736.
        MARIE JEANNE - Born 1 October 1736.

JACQUE TARASCON
    MARIE AVRIL - Native of Tourny in Bourgogne, diocese of Sens.

PIERRE TELLIER - Master turner; died 9 December 1747.
    MARIE ANNE JOURNET (GUERINIE)
        MARIE JOSEPHE - Born 12 January 1728.
        PIERRE THEODORE - Born 18 October 1730.

LOUIS - Born 21 March 1733; buried 3 June 1733.
MARGUERITE LOUISE - Born 6 October 1734.

ETIENNE TESSIER - Sergeant in De La Tour's company; married 18 September 1725.
MAGDELAINE RENEE - Natural daughter of De Mandeville; buried 1 April 1733.
(Daughter) - Baptized 8 November 1725.
ETIENNE - Baptized 5 January 1727.
ETIENNE CLAUDE - Baptized 4 January 1729.
JEAN BAPTISTE - Born 20 May 1731; buried 4 August 1737.

JACQUE THALON - Drummer; buried 15 July 1742.

FRANCOIS THEBRE - Master blacksmith, employed by the Company.
BARBE BENITE
PIERRE - Born 23 December 1726.

RAYMOND GUILLAUME COQUELIN TIOLAIS - Captain of the king's vessel; died 9 February 1755.

JEAN PHILIPPE TIZON - Shoemaker; native of St. Germain en Laye; died 18 August 1746.

NOEL TONDREAUT - Swiss soldier in Karrer's regiment; died 2 January 1750.

JACQUES TORBILLIER - Died 20 August 1751.

TORTILLET
MARIE CLAIRE LE CLERE - Died 4 January 1750.

LOUIS TOUSANGE
JEANNE TOURNAY
JEAN BAPTISTE - Baptized 12 September 1724.

JEAN FRANCOIS TRABAUD - Son of Etienne Trabaud and Marguerite Ordy; native of Boutin; died 4 August 1751.

MATHIEU TREISNAC - Died 3 July 1767.

CLAUDE TREPANIER - Merchant at Fort Louis; Bourgeois at Fort Louis.
GENEVIEVE BUREL

GENEVIEVE - Born 5 February 1709.
MARIE FRANCOISE - Born 25 March 1715.
FRANCOIS - Born 26 February 1717.
BARBE URSULE - Born 28 October 1720.

JEAN CHARLES TROUILLET - Guardian of the storehouse for the king at Allibamons; died while coming to Mobile from his post, 3 October 1752; native of Paris, parish of Ste. Marguerite.

FRANCOIS TRUCHON - Soldier; native of Paris, parish of St. Eustache; buried 24 October 1760.

FRANCOIS TRUDAUT - Habitant of Fort Louis; habitant of Dauphine Island.
    JEANNE BURELLE
        MARIE - Born 17 March 1708.
        JEANNE CATHERINE - Born 28 May 1709.
        FRANCOIS MARIE - Born 31 January 1715.

JEAN VACRIS dit CARIGNAN - Soldier in Le Sueur's company; native of Carignant; son of Jean Vacris; arrived in the colony in 1729; buried 20 June 1740.

JEAN BAPTISTE VALADE dit DRAPEAU LE NOIR - Deceased by 5 May 1722.
    MARIE LE MIR
        JEAN BAPTISTE - Born 5 May 1722; died 25 February 1751.

JEAN VALLADE dit DRAPEAU - Habitant of Fort Louis.
    MARIE PASCOT
        PETRONILLE - Born 29 November 1714.
        MARIE CATHERINE - Born 11 November 1716.
        HENRIETTE - Born 9 June 1718.

SAMUEL VASSEROT - Native of Venay, canton of Berne, Switzerland; Swiss soldier; buried 21 January 1738.

PIERRE VAUTIER - Second-surgeon of the Company; Surgeon-major.
    FRANCOISE PACO (PAQUOT)
        LOUIS MARIE - Born 14 April 1723.
        MARIE LOUISE - Born 19 February 1726.
        FRANCOIS PHILIPPE - Born 16 February 1729.

JOSEPH VEICHER - Swiss soldier; buried 14 August 1760.

JEAN VEILLE
    MARIE JACQUES DE FRANCE
        MARIE FRANCOISE - Born 21 February 1718.
        JEAN PIERRE - Born 12 December 1721.

PIERRE VERNEUIL - Soldier.
    ANNE GUILLET
        MARIE HYACINTHE - Baptized 1 March 1725.
        MARIE ANNE - Baptized 7 January 1732.

VERSCHURS DE TERREPUY - Captain of a detached company of the Marine; died 7 August 1745.

ANDRE VERSIAN dit LA FORTUNE - Soldier in Bertet's company; native of Lhoitat, bishopric of Metz; son of Nicholas Andre Versian and Elizabeth Bobine; buried 27 September 1738, about 47 years old.

LOUIS VICHELIEUX - Soldier.
    (NO WIFE LISTED)
        MICHEL - Buried 29 January 1762.

JACQUES VIEGUELER - Swiss soldier in a detached company of Karrer's regiment; died 27 March 1748, after having made abjuration of Luther's heresy and received the sacraments of the church.

JEAN VIEUILLE
    MARIE DAVID
        JEAN JACQUES - Born 25 January 1721.

PIERRE VIFVAREINE - Sergeant at Fort Louis.
    GABRIELLE SAVARY
        JEAN BAPTISTE - Born 25 February 1719.

NICOLAS VILDREQUIN - Soldier; corporal.
    THERESE JOSEPHE GALLIER (GALIEN) - Died 3 April 1736.
        JEAN - Baptized 26 August 1727.

BAPTISTE VOLAN - Master canoneer for the king; died 18 May 1762.

ELEANOR WALSH - Died 9 October 1766.

ZIBERT (HUBERT) WEISENBACH - Native of Rochach in Switzerland; sergeant in the Swiss troops, company of Grondel; died 12 August 1755, 53 years old.

ANNE MARIE LAMBERDINE LAMBERT - Native of Givé in Flanders; died 28 January 1754.

LORANT CONRAD WILSS (WILTS) - Joiner; native of Esnacin, Saxony. On 9 January 1735, Father Mathias accepted his profession of faith and absolved him of excommunication; died 2 September 1747.

MARIE COLON
MARIE MARGUERITE - Baptized 29 November 1737. (Note: One MARIE ANNE WILTZ died 31 January 1749. No relationship is indicated.)

JEAN WOLFGANG - Soldier in the Fourth Company of Halleville's Swiss company; native of Oberhofen in the Black Forest; buried 15 April 1755.

JOSEPH WOLGUEMONTE - Swiss soldier in the Third company of Karrer's regiment; died 3 February 1748.

GILBERT YANZEN dit ST. SLOY - Soldier in Hazur's company; died 3 December 1747.

THE PRIESTS

The coast was beginning to support permanent settlers when, in 1741, Father Amand, a Capucin priest, wrote: "This church, never having been dedicated, and having been newly rebuilt, we blessed it on the birthday of the Holy Virgin and dedicated it to the Holy Virgin by private commission sent to us by the Reverend Father Pierre, Capucin, Vicar-General of the Monseigneur of Quebec, who ordered us to commemorate the day each year."

Such were the highlights of the priests' year, as they labored in Louisiana — some with extraordinary dedication, others only under orders. Daily routine, however, included caring for the spiritual needs of the congregation, a community that might stretch from Pensacola to New Orleans! The following is a list of priests who served the Gulf Coast area, as revealed in the typescripts on which this volume is based.

The date indicates the year the name first appeared.

1704: Davion
H. Roulleaux De la Vente
Alexandre Huvè
1707: Frere Le Maire
1713: Varlet
1721: Jean Mathieu
Pere Charle
1723: Frere Claude
1725: N. J. de Beaubois
1726: Raphael de Luxembourg
Mathias de Sedan
1727: M. Le Petit
1728: Victorin Dupui
1733: Pierre Vitry
1736: Jean Francois
Francois Guillaume
Morand
1737: Frere Prosper
Frere Felix
1738: Frere Agnan
Frere Amand
1743: Frere Seraphin
1747: Frere Pierre
1753: Frere Sebastien
Frere Barnabé
1756: Frere Ferdinand

INDEX

Alexandre 23, 45, 56
Arlu 25, 52, 59
Avril 47, 60

Bacque 47
Balivet 31
Basile 41
Baudouin 32
Benite 61
Bernard 18, 28
Bernoudy 18
Bienvenue 36
Blaise 49
Bodin 17
Boissinot 35, 46
Bouche 36
Bouly 44
Bourgeois 28
Boyer 33, 41, 49
Brenard 25
Bret 18, 19, 45
Brett 59
Brignac 54
Brochon 24, 28
Brouin 28
Bruyard 56
Burel 29, 61
Burelle 62

Candrague 48
Cesteri 42
Chabert 21
Chagneau 28
Chatelier 29
Chatellier 29, 56
Chauvin 30, 33
Chenet 25, 56
Chevy 56
Christophe 17
Claudine 32
Colon 17, 41, 42, 57, 64
Colpe 48
Corhuel 48

Cornuel 48
Cotter 51

Daniau 40
D'Arleu 37
Darnelle 52
David 63
De Beranhard 31
De Bourasse 32
De France 63
De Fresne 20
De La Fond 37
De La Vergne 26
De Loumeau 43
De Lusser 30
De Molondron 30
De Remont 29
De Robec 55
De St. Michel 47
De St. Simon 31
Des Fontaine 34
Des Hayes 23
Des Orges 49, 55
De Vallee 21, 32
De Vaudezare 31
Doussin 59
Drouin 28
Dufrene 17
Du Fresne 17, 20
Du Pre 30
Duvalle 31
Du Vau 36

Ecrivain 60
Estienne 45
Eugene 47
Euger 47
Eulie 56

Farcois [sic] 38
Fasinot 34
Feger 48
Finaux 49

67

Flaye 28
Flein 28
Folle 37
Font 37
Foucauld 39
Foucaut 35
Fouiot 59
Fourche 44
Fourchet 47
Francoise 47

Gabriau 19
Gabriel 19
Gabriot 53
Galbrun 34
Galien 63
Gallier 63
Gallion 46
Gallois 52
Garnier 29
Gaultre 51
George 48
Gilbert 58
Girard 50
Girardy 50
Gotte 51
Grandval 30
Grise 37
Grisse 37
Guerinie 60
Guilbert 58
Guillaume 49
Guillet 34, 63
Guillette 27

Henry 38
Heuger 47
Houssau 23
Housseau 20
Huet 21
Hussot 53

Jalbren 42
Jallot 24, 25
Journee 47
Journet 60
Jouso 59

Jouvillinac 19

Kerouest 35
King 45

Labrau 58
La Breau 58
La Brosse 58
La Case 40
La Casse 60
La Fond 28, 34, 53
Lafont 28
La Fontaine 28, 34
La Marre 51
Lambert 64
Lami 18
L'Ami 26
Lamie 51
Lamy 26, 39
Lange 58
Lani 18
Lanier 26
Laplace 54
La Pointe 43
Larieux 55
Layie 39
Le Clere 61
L'Ecrue 50
Le Febvre 32
Le Maire 54
Le Mir 18, 21, 38, 62
Lemire 47
Le Moine 50
Le Page 28
Le Sueur 43
Lisle 53
Luvat 58

Maginet 55
Mahou 45
Mahould 45
Manseau 32
Martin 58
Megard 28
Mercier 20, 26
Meri 31
Meusuier 55

Nadeout 42
Naula 58
Nota 58

Ouanet 36

Paco 62
Paillet 22
Panyoussa 21
Paquot 62
Pascot 62
Peaux 41
Perot 55
Philippe 41, 58
Pierre 25
Poirier 23
Potier 53
Pouillot 48
Prau 27, 54
Praux 41, 60
Preau 27, 34
Prevost 53
Prieur 25
Prot 17, 27, 60

Quentin 19
Quervegan 42
Quirioles 46

Real 41
Reinne 41
Remond 29
Renee 51, 61
Richard 52
Robert 25, 44
Rochon 32
Rocques 50
Roge 36
Roger 24
Roque 18
Roquet 50
Rosno 51
Rouget 24
Rousseau 46
Roy 55
Rualland 51
Ruellant 22
Ruiso 51

St. Lazare 33
Sarrasin 57
Savary 59, 63
Senche 56
Simon 43
Sulivan 18

Tabouret 39
Tachoune 19
Talon 51
Tanca 45
Thibaut 29
Tienne 45
Tiensa 45
Tieu 45
Toulouse 20
Tournay 61
Trudot 43
Turpin 58

Utsiger 41

Valde 32
Valdre 35
Valene 34
Valois 34
Vallon 34
Vallone 34, 52
Valon 34
Valone 34
Valter 43
Valtere 24
Vergne 19, 40
Veu 21
Vilaine 44
Vinconnau 20
Vivier 46
Volant 40
Vualdre 32

Walte 32
Waltre 32

www.ingramcontent.com/pod-product-compliance
Lightning Source LLC
Chambersburg PA
CBHW070518090426
42735CB00012B/2835